Still Standing
A Journey Through Trauma, Survival and Grace

Karen Kazimer Shockley

Karens Words

Copyright © 2025 Karen Shockley

All rights reserved

The characters and events portrayed in this book are fictitious. Any similarity to real persons, living or dead, is coincidental and not intended by the author.

No part of this book may be reproduced, or stored in a retrieval system, or transmitted in any form or by any means, electronic, mechanical, photocopying, recording, or otherwise, without express written permission of the publisher.

Printed in the United States of America

A MOTHER'S PRAYER

My Precious Children,

There are so many things I want to tell you—more than I could ever fit into a single letter. But today, I simply want to speak from my heart and remind you how deeply you are loved.

From the moment I first saw you, I knew my life had changed forever. You brought purpose, laughter, and a kind of love I didn't know was possible. I've watched you grow, stumble, laugh, and learn—and through it all, I've prayed that you always feel how cherished you are.

Life won't always be easy. You'll face disappointments, questions, and moments when you might feel lost. But I want you to remember this: You are never truly alone. My love goes with you always, and God's grace surrounds you—even when you can't feel it.

Be kind. Be brave. Do your best. Forgive quickly. Say "I love you" often. And never forget that who you are is far more important than what you do.

I am so proud of you—for being real. For growing. For showing up with your whole heart.

If you ever doubt your worth, come back to this letter. Let it remind you:

You are my heart.

You are my legacy.

And you are deeply, unshakably loved.

With all the love in the world,

Mom

For every woman who has cried alone in the dark,
who stayed too long,
who loved too deeply,
and who blamed herself for surviving.

This is for you.

You are not weak.
You are not forgotten.
You are not alone.

May this story remind you that no matter what you've endured,
you are still worthy of love, still worthy of peace,
and still standing by the grace of God.

CONTENTS

Title Page
Copyright
A Mother's Prayer
Dedication
Chapter 1: A Good Girl — 1
Chapter 2: Love, Marriage, Warning — 5
— 7
Chapter 3: The Razor and the Dog — 10
— 12
Chapter 4: The System Failed Us — 15
— 17
Chapter 5: The Kids I Couldn't Save — 21
— 23
Chapter 6: Under the Bridge — 27
— 29
Chapter 7: When Grace Found Me — 32
— 34
Chapter 8: Why I Still Pray — 37
Chapter 9: What I Would Tell Her Now — 41
— 43

Chapter 10: Still Standing	46
	48
Questions for the Reader	50
Chapter 1 – A Good Girl	51
Chapter 2 – Love, Marriage, and Warning Signs	52
Chapter 3 – The Razor and the Dog	53
Chapter 4 – The System Failed Us	54
Chapter 5 – The Kids I Couldn't Save	55
Chapter 6 – Under the Bridge	56
Chapter 7 – When Grace Found Me	57
Chapter 8 – Why I Still Pray	58
Chapter 9 – What I Would Tell Her Now	59
Chapter 10 – Still Standing	60
PRAYERS FOR INNER PEACE	61
Prayer for Peace at Night	62
Prayer for Guilt	63
Prayer for Her Children	64
Prayer for Strength	65
Prayer for Protection	66
Prayer for Clarity	67
Prayer of Thankfulness	68
Prayer for Forgiveness	69
Prayer for Comfort	70
Prayer for Healing	71
Prayer for Purpose	72
Prayer for Courage	73
Prayer for Joy	74
Prayer for Faith	75

Prayer for Trust	76
Prayer for Her Younger Self	77
Prayer for Her Future	78
Prayer for Other Women Like Her	79
Prayer for Rest	80
Prayer of Praise	81
Epilogue	83
Books By This Author	89

CHAPTER 1: A GOOD GIRL

"Who can find a virtuous woman? for her price is far above rubies."
— Proverbs 31:10 (KJV)

I was always the good girl. I was the one who said, "thank you" and "please." The one who didn't speak out of turn. The one who held the door open for strangers and didn't cut in line, even when I was in a hurry. I did what was expected of me, and then I did a little more. I baked for the church potluck. I kept my promises. I remembered birthdays. I apologized first, even when I wasn't wrong.

Because that's what good girls do.

Growing up, I believed in the golden rule. I clung to it the way some children hold a blanket to their chest at night—tight and trembling. I thought if I just did everything *right*, life would be kind in return. That was the silent contract, wasn't it? Be good, and you'll be safe. Be kind, and kindness will find you.

But life didn't sign that contract.

Still, I tried. I tried so hard to be a good daughter. A good student. A good Christian. Later, a good wife. A good mother. I poured myself into those roles until there was barely anything left of *me*—just a tired shape molded by expectations and driven by duty. And I didn't question it. I didn't pause. I didn't say, "What about me?" Because I didn't think I was allowed to.

My parents raised me to believe that strength meant silence, that grace meant never complaining. So, I became strong in all the wrong ways. I swallowed sadness. I smiled through confusion. I soothed everyone else's wounds while hiding my own.

And I believed—I truly believed—that God was pleased with

me. That Heaven kept a tally of all the times I'd bitten my tongue or offered forgiveness when fury would have been easier. I thought maybe God loved good girls more than messy ones. I thought goodness would save me from the storm.

But storms don't check your resume.

When the darkest chapter of my life began, all of that obedience—all of that striving—felt like a joke. Where was my shield? Where was my reward? I had been so careful. So faithful. So good.

And yet I was about to die. At the hands of a man I had once loved. In a house I had tried so hard to make safe. With my children just a room away.

The girl I had been—the girl who believed good people were spared—was about to meet the truth: that evil can still find you, that mental illness doesn't play fair, and that even when you do everything "right," the world can still come crashing down.

But she was also about to discover something even deeper: that being *good* isn't the same as being *faithful*. And that God's grace doesn't depend on how many rules you follow—but how many times you reach for Him when you have nothing else to give.

This is the story of the girl I was—and the woman God is still shaping me to be.

One breath. One breakdown. One prayer at a time.

CHAPTER 2: LOVE, MARRIAGE, WARNING

"Trust in the Lord with all thine heart; and lean not unto thine own understanding. In all thy ways acknowledge him, and he shall direct thy paths."
— Proverbs 3:5–6 (KJV)

We met young, like so many do. He was funny, charming, and quick-witted. He had a way of making me feel seen—like I was special, like he had found something in me that no one else had noticed. And I, in all my eagerness to build a life and a future, clung to that feeling like it was truth.

The wedding was simple. A few flowers, a handful of family, a promise spoken before God. I believed in vows. I believed in forever. I believed that love was enough.

I didn't understand then that love isn't a cure—not for mental illness, not for fear, not for a heart already at war with itself.

The signs were there, even in the beginning. The mood swings. The quiet disappearances. The angry silence that followed the most innocent question. But I didn't see them for what they were. I was taught to be loyal. To be patient. To believe that everyone had good in them, and that love—if strong enough—could fix what was broken.

There were times of tenderness, of course. That's what makes it so confusing. He could be kind. He could be brilliant. He made me laugh in a way no one else ever had. And when things were good, they were very good. But like a glass that catches the light just right, I now realize: the beautiful parts distracted me from the crack running through the center.

After our first child was born, things shifted. There was pressure, and he didn't handle it well. The weight of responsibility—fatherhood, finances, the reality of adulthood—it seemed to unravel something inside him. He began to retreat into his own mind. Conversations became arguments. Arguments became silence. And silence became dread.

There were nights I lay awake beside him, staring at the ceiling, wondering who he really was—and if the man I married was still in there somewhere. I told myself it was stress. I told myself all marriages were hard. I told myself it would pass.

But it didn't pass.

The darkness grew thicker, the episodes more unpredictable. There were days he wouldn't come out of the bedroom. Other days he would pace, muttering under his breath, eyes darting toward shadows I couldn't see. I remember once asking him what was wrong and being met with a blank stare, like I was the stranger in the house, not him.

Still, I stayed.

I stayed because I believed in vows. I stayed because of the children. I stayed because the church said marriage was forever. I stayed because I was ashamed to admit I might have made a mistake.

But mostly, I stayed because I thought God would fix it—if I prayed hard enough, served long enough, loved deeply enough.

What I didn't understand then is that God doesn't call us to sacrifice ourselves on the altar of someone else's brokenness.

There is a difference between carrying someone's burden and being buried under it.

Looking back, I wish someone had told me that boundaries can be holy. That leaving doesn't mean you don't love. That protection is not abandonment. That rescuing yourself—especially when children are involved—is not failure. It is wisdom. It is courage.

It is survival.

I didn't know that then.

But I was about to learn.

CHAPTER 3: THE RAZOR AND THE DOG

"Yea, though I walk through the valley of the shadow of death, I will fear no evil: for thou art with me..."
— Psalm 23:4 (KJV)

It happened on a Thursday.

I don't know why that matters. Maybe because the ordinariness of the day makes the memory more unbearable. There were dishes in the sink. A load of laundry half-folded. The kids—eight and six—were watching cartoons in the living room. Our dog, Spot, was curled up nearby, tail twitching in his sleep.

And I was in the bedroom with my husband.

I can't remember what we were talking about before it started. Maybe nothing. Maybe everything. With him, there were no warnings—just shifts. Sudden, cold shifts in energy, as though a storm blew through the windows without opening them.

One moment we were speaking. The next, he was standing over me with a straight edge razor in his hand.

The light in his eyes was gone. In its place there was something empty, something lost. He didn't yell. He didn't scream. He spoke softly, almost with sorrow, as if delivering a grim but necessary truth.

"They're coming for you," he said. "They're going to hurt you. I have to stop it before it happens. I have to save you."

I froze. My mind tried to make sense of the words, but they didn't belong in any rational world. He believed it. Whatever voice he'd been listening to in his head, it convinced him that I was in danger—and that *he* was the only one who could save me.

Even if it meant killing me.

I begged him to stop. I told him I loved him. I said the children needed me. But none of it reached him. He was somewhere else—deep in a fog I couldn't enter, led by hallucinations and terror I couldn't see.

Then I screamed.

It wasn't a scream I planned. It came from the deepest part of me—from the corner where survival instinct lives. And that scream woke someone else.

Spot.

Our dog, our faithful mutt with floppy ears and a heart too big for his little body, came flying down the hallway. I heard him slam into the bedroom door, barking wildly, scratching and growling like a wild animal. The door was locked, but it didn't matter. His barking was relentless, desperate. He knew something was wrong.

And by some miracle, the noise broke the trance.

My husband blinked, looked at the razor in his hand, then looked at me. He stepped back. Just enough. I ran past him, unlocked the door, and collapsed into the hallway. Spot was there, barking and jumping, placing himself between me and the danger.

That night, the man I married tried to kill me.

And the dog we adopted from the shelter saved my life.

Later, I would learn that people with untreated schizophrenia and bipolar disorder often experience voices—cruel voices—convincing them that those they love are in danger, and that the only way to protect them is through death. It's a tragic distortion. A heartbreaking lie disguised as salvation. And it almost took everything from me.

The hospital took him in—for a while. He was diagnosed. Medicated. Discharged far too soon. They said he wasn't a threat anymore. They said I'd be safe. That the kids would be fine.

They were wrong.

I wish I could say that moment was the turning point, the place where healing began. But it wasn't. It was only the beginning of a much longer nightmare.

Trauma has a way of taking root—not just in memory, but in your body, in your bones. My children never felt safe again. They scanned every room for exits. They flinched at sudden noises. They waited, always, for the next explosion.

And I—who had spent a lifetime trying to be good—felt like the worst mother in the world.

Because I couldn't protect them.

Because I had let him in.

Because I stayed.

But God stayed, too.

Even when I didn't feel Him. Even when I couldn't pray. Even when I couldn't forgive myself. Somewhere in the thick of it, there was still a presence holding me together.

I just didn't know yet that it was grace.

CHAPTER 4: THE SYSTEM FAILED US

"The Lord is nigh unto them that are of a broken heart; and saveth such as be of a contrite spirit."
— Psalm 34:18 (KJV)

They said it was safe.

They looked at me with calm voices and clinical words and told me that he could come home. That the medication was working. That the danger had passed.

They were wrong.

They didn't see my children clutching each other under the kitchen table whenever a door slammed. They didn't feel the tension in the house—the sharp edge of every breath. They didn't understand that Haldol might dull the mania but did nothing to fix the fracture in our foundation.

What they did was release a man who had just tried to kill me with a straight edge razor, back into the home where our children were still learning how to spell the word "danger."

Six months of in-home therapy followed. Counselors came and went. Charts were made. Sessions were held. But the truth was this: they treated the symptoms, not the fear. And fear was what we lived with every single day.

I watched my children become shadows. They were always scanning—rooms, faces, moods. They were learning how to disappear, how to be small, how to read every micro expression on their father's face to gauge whether or not today would end in peace or panic.

My son started keeping a flashlight and a pair of shoes by his bed. Just in case. My daughter flinched if anyone raised their voice—even in laughter. They didn't feel safe in their own home, and nothing I did could convince them otherwise. Because I couldn't believe it either.

I couldn't sleep. I couldn't eat. Every sound felt like a threat. I kept knives out of reach, locked bedroom doors, stayed half-dressed just in case I had to run. That's not what a home is supposed to be.

And still, I stayed.

I told myself it was the right thing. That I was honoring my vows. That if I just tried harder, prayed harder, loved harder, this brokenness would finally heal.

But the healing didn't come.

The system told me to be patient. To give it time. That families "heal together." But what about when healing together means reopening the wound again and again? What about when together means terror?

No one told me that sometimes the Godliest thing you can do is walk away. That God doesn't ask us to martyr ourselves to save someone else. That protecting your children is not rebellion. It is righteousness.

Still, I waited four years to leave.

Four years of pretending. Four years of fear. Four years of my children growing up in a war zone disguised as a living room.

When I finally filed for divorce, I felt like I had failed God. The church wasn't kind. Friends disappeared. Whispers replaced compassion. I was seen as the woman who gave up—when in reality, I had held on far too long.

Justin wouldn't go quietly. The paranoia had taken root. He

stopped trusting anyone. Refused help. Eventually, he lived under a bridge. Cold. Alone. Convinced the world was out to get him.

And then… he died.

It was a quiet death. No drama. No headline. Just another man with mental illness who slipped through the cracks. Another statistic buried under a system that never truly helped.

I didn't weep at the funeral. I wept in private, in pieces, over years.

The kids reacted in their own ways. One erased him from their memory entirely. Like he never existed. The second carried guilt like a stone in their pocket—too heavy to hold, too familiar to let go.

And me?

I tried to rebuild. But the damage had sunk deep. And every time I looked at my children's pain, I heard the same voice in my mind:

"You couldn't protect them."

The system failed us. But worse—I believed I had failed them, too.

It would take many more years, and more heartache than I care to name, before I would begin to see a different truth: that I did the best I could with what I had… and that God was not blaming me.

He was carrying me.

Even in silence.

Even in shame.

Even in the collapse.

Grace had not left. It was just waiting for me to stop trying to save everyone else—and finally let it save me.

CHAPTER 5: THE KIDS I COULDN'T SAVE

"And he shall wipe away all tears from their eyes; and there shall be no more death, neither sorrow, nor crying, neither shall there be any more pain..."
— Revelation 21:4 (KJV)

I used to watch them sleep—my children—and wonder if they'd ever feel safe again.

The way their little chests rose and fell. The way one clutched a stuffed animal like a lifeline. The way the other always slept facing the door, as if guarding the room. Sleep was their only refuge. But even that, sometimes, was interrupted by nightmares.

And I was the one who let the danger in.

It's a lie, of course. I didn't invite the madness. I didn't cause the illness. I didn't carve the cracks into their hearts. But when you are a mother, pain becomes your inheritance—and their suffering, your indictment.

I tried everything. Therapy. Church. Art programs. Music lessons. Picnics in the park. I wrapped normalcy around them like a blanket, desperate to make them feel what I no longer did: safe, secure, loved.

But trauma doesn't yield to bedtime stories. It doesn't dissolve with macaroni art or hugs. It lingers. It burrows. It rewrites the brain's idea of "normal."

My older became quiet, too quiet. Hyper-vigilant. Always assessing. Always planning an escape route. He'd sit with his back to the wall, just like a soldier. I found out years later he never went into a public building without scanning for exits.

My younger child turned inward. Shame became a second skin. She blamed herself for things no child should. She carried guilt like duty, trying to be the good one, the calm one, the one who wouldn't break the way everything else had. When she smiled, I saw the sadness behind her eyes like smoke behind glass.

Each of them bore the trauma differently, but they both carried it—like invisible backpacks too heavy for children to wear. And me? I tried to carry *them*. All of them. All the time.

But I couldn't.

I can't explain the ache of watching your child flinch when you raise your voice in laughter. Or seeing their eyes go dark when you say a phrase their father once used. I can't explain what it feels like to tell a school counselor, "Please don't say the word *father* in class today. My son won't make it through."

I tried to protect them. But what do you do when the danger sleeps down the hall? What do you do when the very person you promised would love and guard them is the one who left scars they still bleed from in secret?

You do what mothers do. You keep going.

You cry in the shower. You pray through gritted teeth. You forgive yourself a hundred times a day and still carry the guilt into bed at night.

You show up, even when you're broken.

You pack lunches and drive to therapy and say things like "You're safe now" even when you're not sure it's true.

I failed them.

That's what I believed for years. It echoed louder than any compliment, drowned out every attempt at healing. I failed them.

But slowly—so slowly—I began to learn something I didn't

know when I was trying so hard to be the perfect mother:

Faith doesn't require you to be perfect. It requires you to keep showing up.

Some days, I just showed up.

Some days, that was enough.

There were moments when my children, older now, would say something that stopped me cold. Something kind. Something human. A thank you. A soft laugh. A memory not entirely filled with dread. And in those moments, I saw that maybe I hadn't failed completely.

Maybe they saw me trying. Maybe they saw love, even when it came through tears.

Maybe survival, in the end, *was* the proof of love.

And maybe—just maybe—God was healing all of us, one cracked, grace-soaked piece at a time.

Maybe survival, in the end, *was* the proof of love.

And maybe—just maybe—God was healing all of us, one cracked, grace-soaked piece at a time.

CHAPTER 6: UNDER THE BRIDGE

"Come unto me, all ye that labor and are heavy laden, and I will give you rest."
— Matthew 11:28 (KJV)

By the time he was living under the bridge, he no longer recognized me.

The man who once promised to protect me—the man who once held our children in his arms and whispered lullabies—was now a ghost with skin. He had slipped so far into paranoia that even kindness felt like an attack. He trusted no one, not even himself.

Mental illness had devoured what was left of him. Not just his mind, but his dignity, his ability to reason, his capacity to care for himself. He wandered the city with a plastic bag full of tattered notebooks and old receipts, convinced that "they" were coming. He'd stopped taking his meds long before that. He said they were poison. He said I was part of it.

He called sometimes—on borrowed phones, in broken sentences. Sometimes he'd accuse me of things I didn't understand. Other times he'd cry and beg me to come get him, but when I tried, he'd disappear. I'd drive the streets, looking for him. Not because I still loved him, but because I once did. Because he was the father of my children. Because I still carried the echo of the vow I'd made decades ago.

Because I still saw the man he had been.

But love is not a cure, and guilt is not a compass.

Eventually, the calls stopped. Word came from someone who had seen him—said he was sleeping in the weeds near the overpass, barely clothed, mumbling scripture and fragments of songs from our youth. Then even those sightings faded.

When the call finally came—that he was gone—I didn't cry right away. I sat very still, holding the phone in one hand and a coffee cup in the other. I stared out the window, not sure if what I felt was sorrow or relief.

He died alone. Cold. Probably confused.

I talked to the children. One didn't say much. He had long since severed the emotional cord. For him, he'd already been dead for years. He had grieved in advance, then walked away to preserve what was left of themselves.

The second? The one who still carried the weight of memory and guilt? She wept. Not because he died, but because she never got the ending they hoped for. No reconciliation. No explanation. Just silence.

It's one thing to survive trauma. It's another to lose the person who caused it without ever hearing them say, "I'm sorry."

And so we sat, each of us, in our separate corners of grief. I lit a candle that night—not for the man he became, but for the boy he once was. The one who dreamed of being a pilot. The one who loved poetry. The one who danced with me barefoot in the kitchen on our first anniversary. That boy had died a long time ago. Now, the body had followed.

For a long time, I thought forgiveness meant pretending it didn't hurt. That healing meant erasing the story. But that's not what faith taught me. Faith taught me to hold both truth and grace in the same hand. To weep for what was lost and still thank God for what was spared.

I will never understand the fullness of what broke inside him.

I will never make peace with the scars he left behind. But I will no longer carry his actions as evidence of my failure.

He is gone. And I am still here.

I'm here because of a barking dog and a thousand mercies I didn't deserve.

I'm here because somewhere in the ruin, I found a God who did not abandon me—who sat in the ashes with me, weeping when I wept, lifting me when I couldn't move, whispering life back into places I thought were permanently dead.

He died under a bridge.

But I didn't.

I lived.

And that is a miracle I won't waste.

CHAPTER 7: WHEN GRACE FOUND ME

"For I know the thoughts that I think toward you, saith the Lord, thoughts of peace, and not of evil, to give you an expected end."
—Jeremiah 29:11 (KJV)

I didn't have a dramatic salvation moment. There was no thunderclap, no blinding light, no sudden falling to my knees in a church aisle. Grace didn't roar into my life. It crept in, gently—like the way morning sunlight spills across a dark room, touching everything before you even notice it's arrived.

I was sixty-two when I told God I wanted to die.

I sat on the edge of my bed, knees aching, hands clasped so tightly they turned white. There was no one left in the house. No more therapy appointments. No court dates. No panic alarms by the bed. Just the silence of a life that had been ripped apart and stitched back together too many times.

I whispered, "I can't do this anymore."

And in that quiet moment—when even hope had packed its bags and left—something stirred in my spirit. Not a voice. Not a sign. Just… a presence.

A stillness that didn't feel empty.

A warmth that didn't come from the heater.

A nudge in my soul that said, *I see you.*

And for the first time in a long time, I cried without shame. Not out of guilt. Not out of grief. But because I felt something holy sitting beside me. Not judging. Not fixing. Just *being there*.

That's when I knew I hadn't been forgotten.

God hadn't looked away in my suffering. He had been there in every hallway I paced. In every locked door. In every courtroom seat. In every whispered prayer I couldn't finish. In every child's trembling hand I held. In every scream that went unanswered—He had been *there*.

Grace didn't erase my past.

It reframed it.

I stopped seeing myself as the worst mother in the world. I started seeing myself as a woman who had endured hell and still held her children through it. A woman who stayed when it was dangerous and left when it was right. A woman who fed her babies even when her soul was starving. A woman who was wounded, yes—but also faithful.

I let the word "survivor" land on my skin and didn't flinch.

I read the Bible again—not like a checklist, but like a letter. I lingered in Psalms. I clung to Romans 8. I let the story of Hagar remind me that even in the wilderness, God is the God who sees.

And little by little, I came back to life.

Not in the way I expected.

Not all at once.

But slowly, like winter surrendering to spring.

There were still hard days. Grief doesn't ask for your permission, and healing doesn't mean forgetting. But I learned how to hold beauty and sorrow in the same breath. How to laugh without guilt. How to hope without fear.

How to trust that my story—*even this story*—could still be used for good.

Not as a cautionary tale. Not as a tragedy. But as a testimony.

Because here's the thing: I thought my life was over.

But God wasn't finished yet.

CHAPTER 8: WHY I STILL PRAY

"The effectual fervent prayer of a righteous man availeth much."
— James 5:16 (KJV)

There was a long stretch of my life when prayer felt like screaming into a void.

I prayed when my children cried themselves to sleep. I prayed when the man I loved turned into someone I didn't recognize. I prayed when the locks on the doors didn't feel strong enough. And then, after a while, I stopped praying at all.

Not because I stopped believing in God.
But because I believed He had stopped listening.

I thought prayer was a transaction. That if I said the right words with the right heart, God would move. And when He didn't move the way I asked, I assumed it was my failure. My sin. My punishment.

I carried shame into every prayer like a shadow.

But grace—oh, grace—it changed everything.

Grace whispered that prayer wasn't about getting it right.
It was about *showing up*.
Even broken.
Especially broken.

I started praying again. Not eloquently. Not confidently. But honestly.

"God, I'm here. I don't know what to say."

"God, I'm angry, but I need You."

"God, I'm tired, but I trust You."

"God, help me breathe."

There's something sacred about whispering to Heaven when you feel like you're barely holding on. Those were the prayers that healed me—not because they changed my situation, but because they changed *me*.

Prayer became less about answers and more about presence.

I started seeing God in places I had overlooked: in the morning light through the window, in the laughter of my grandchild, in the unexpected phone call from a friend. He was never far. I had just stopped looking.

Now, prayer is my anchor.

I pray not because life is easy, but because I've seen what happens when I try to carry it alone.

I pray for my children—the grown versions who are still healing in quiet, complicated ways. I pray for other women like me, sitting in houses that no longer feel like homes. I pray for the tired ones, the silent ones, the survivors who don't know if they deserve peace.

I pray because peace is not earned. It's given.

I pray because I've learned that God can handle our raw. Our messy. Our angry. Our silent. He doesn't need perfection. He just wants presence.

And every time I speak to Him now—even in the simplest way—I imagine Him saying back to me:

"I've been here all along."

CHAPTER 9: WHAT I WOULD TELL HER NOW

"He healeth the broken in heart, and bindeth up their wounds."
— Psalm 147:3 (KJV)

If I could go back and sit beside the woman I used to be—the version of me curled up on the bathroom floor, too tired to cry, too ashamed to pray—I wouldn't scold her.
I wouldn't give her advice.

I wouldn't quote Scripture like a Band-Aid.

I would just hold her hand.

And after a long, quiet while, I'd whisper the words she needed most:

"You didn't deserve this."

Not the violence.
Not the betrayal.
Not the silence from people who should have helped.
Not the guilt you were made to carry for other people's decisions.

You were a mother doing her best.
A woman with a heart too big and a hope too stubborn to let go.
You loved as fiercely as you could in a house built on shifting sand.
And when the storm came, you didn't run.
You stayed and held your children through the shaking.
Then you picked up the pieces and rebuilt what you could with trembling hands.

You thought you failed.

But I know better now.

You didn't fail.

You survived.

You adapted.

You kept the lights on and the meals coming.
You gave your children something to believe in—even if it was just the steady rhythm of your footsteps down the hallway at night.
You were the net that caught the falling.
You were the roof when the world cracked open.
You were their only safe place.

And you did all of that while carrying your own heartbreak like a hidden wound.

I would tell her:
You were not weak for crying.
You were strong for getting back up.
You were not broken beyond repair.
You were being rebuilt by the hands of mercy.

And I would say this:

"God was never ashamed of you. Not once."

Not when you stopped praying.

Not when you doubted Him.

Not when you said, "I want to die."

He was there, even then.
Holding your soul together with grace invisible to your eyes.
Waiting. Not impatiently. But faithfully.
Because He knew… someday, you would begin to see yourself the way He always had.

Loved.

Held.
Redeemed.

And I think she—broken, breathless, unbelieving me—might lift her eyes just enough to say:

"…Really?"

And I'd smile and say:

"Yes. Really. You are the story He's still telling."

CHAPTER 10: STILL STANDING

"Now unto him that is able to keep you from falling, and to present you faultless before the presence of his glory with exceeding joy..."
—Jude 1:24 (KJV)

I am still here.
Old. Wrinkled, weathered, and still standing.
Not because life was gentle with me.
Not because I did everything right.
Not because I was strong enough.

But because grace caught me when I couldn't stand on my own.

There are scars—yes. Wounds that don't fully heal. But scars mean healing has happened. They are the proof I bled, and the proof I survived. I used to hide them. Now, I name them like altars—each one a place where God met me in the wreckage and stayed.

I am not the same woman I once was.
She was afraid of breaking.
I have learned that brokenness is where the light gets in.

I once thought my story was one of loss.
Now I know it's one of resurrection.

I thought I would die from heartbreak.
But I have lived—*truly lived*—through the ashes.

My children still carry pieces of what we walked through. I won't pretend that faith made everything easy. It didn't erase the pain. But it gave us a framework to keep building. A way to hold sorrow and beauty at the same time. A path back to one another, even in silence.

We are not perfect.
We are not untouched.
But we are still a family.

And I am still their mother.

There are women reading this now who are where I was.
Tired. Guilty. Fractured by trauma.
You feel like your story ended years ago, and you're just turning pages in a book with no more plot.
But I am here to say:

God is not finished.

You are not too old.
You are not too broken.
You are not too late.

There is still breath in your lungs.
There is still a sunrise waiting for you tomorrow.
And there is a Savior who still calls you *by name.*

You are loved.
You are seen.
You are not forgotten.

This is not the end.

It is only a new beginning.

So take a breath.
Take a step.
And say it with me, even if your voice shakes:

"By the grace of God… I am still standing."

QUESTIONS FOR THE READER

Take your time with responding to these questions. They are meant for journaling, prayer, or quiet contemplation.

CHAPTER 1 – A GOOD GIRL

Have you ever believed that being "good" would protect you from pain? How has that belief shaped your life or relationships?

CHAPTER 2 – LOVE, MARRIAGE, AND WARNING SIGNS

Looking back on your past relationships, were there any early warning signs you overlooked? What would you tell your younger self now?

CHAPTER 3 – THE RAZOR AND THE DOG

Have you ever experienced a moment where you felt completely helpless? What—or who—helped you survive?

CHAPTER 4 – THE SYSTEM FAILED US

Have you ever felt let down by a system or institution you trusted? How did it affect your healing?

CHAPTER 5 – THE KIDS I COULDN'T SAVE

How do you carry guilt—especially in your role as a parent, partner, or caregiver? What truth do you need to speak over that guilt today?

CHAPTER 6 – UNDER THE BRIDGE

What does forgiveness mean to you now? Are there people or moments in your life that still feel unresolved?

CHAPTER 7 – WHEN GRACE FOUND ME

Was there a quiet moment in your life when you realized God had not left you? What did that moment teach you?

CHAPTER 8 – WHY I STILL PRAY

How has your understanding of prayer changed over time? What would your honest, unfiltered prayer sound like today?

CHAPTER 9 – WHAT I WOULD TELL HER NOW

What would you say to the version of yourself who was hurting the most? Write her a letter.

CHAPTER 10 – STILL STANDING

What does "still standing" look like in your life today? How has grace helped you rebuild?

PRAYERS FOR INNER PEACE

PRAYER FOR PEACE AT NIGHT

Lord, calm the storms that still live in my memories.
Let the darkness not awaken fear, but rest.
Replace the echo of trauma with Your whispered peace.
Let my sleep be a sanctuary, not a battlefield.
Wrap me in stillness that speaks of Your love.
Watch over my dreams until morning light.

PRAYER FOR GUILT

Father, take this guilt that weighs so heavy.
I carried it for years, believing it was mine to bear.
But You know my heart—you saw my trying.
Help me believe that my best was enough.
Unshackle me from shame I never earned.
Let me walk forward, lighter in Your grace.

PRAYER FOR HER CHILDREN

Lord, hold my children in Your tender mercy.
Go where my arms cannot reach.
Heal the wounds they still carry quietly.
Let them feel safety, even now.
Redeem what trauma stole from them.
Restore peace to their precious hearts.

PRAYER FOR STRENGTH

On the days I feel too tired to rise,
Remind me that breathing is strength enough.
Let my past be a monument, not a burden.
I am still here—and that matters.
Help me see victory in simply standing.
Strengthen my soul where it still trembles.

PRAYER FOR PROTECTION

Cover me, Lord, with Your sheltering wings.
Let no fear take root in me again.
I've lived too long on edge—
Let me now walk in safety and trust.
Guard my heart, my mind, my rest.
Keep me in perfect peace, I pray.

PRAYER FOR CLARITY

Untangle truth from the knots of my memory.
Help me see with heaven's perspective.
Let me not live ruled by confusion or fear.
Speak light into every dark corner.
Guide me gently back to wisdom.
Let truth bring freedom, not shame.

PRAYER OF THANKFULNESS

Thank You for the grace that came quietly.
For the dog that barked, for the neighbor who checked.
For strength I didn't know I had.
For the moments I was carried, not crushed.
You were there, even when I couldn't see You.
And for that—I will always give thanks.

PRAYER FOR FORGIVENESS

Teach me how to forgive what broke me.
Not to pretend it didn't hurt—
But to release the grip of pain from my soul.
You ask us to forgive, not to forget.
So help me let go without losing wisdom.
And in doing so, find peace again.

PRAYER FOR COMFORT

When silence feels too loud,
When loneliness returns like a shadow,
Be my comfort, Lord.
Sit with me in the emptiness.
Let me feel You close in the stillness.
Be the warmth that steadies my heart.

PRAYER FOR HEALING

Heal the places I've hidden from even myself.
The aches I tucked behind smiles.
The fears that still wake me from sleep.
I give You every shattered place inside.
Rebuild what life tried to destroy.
Make me whole—not perfect—but whole.

PRAYER FOR PURPOSE

God, let this pain not be wasted.
Make it useful, somehow holy.
Turn my story into a light for someone else's night.
Use what was meant for harm to birth healing.
Let my life echo with purpose.
Even now, even still.

PRAYER FOR COURAGE

Give me courage to keep telling the truth.
Even when the world prefers silence.
Let my voice be steady, even if my hands shake.
Remind me that honesty is healing.
Even if it costs comfort, it births freedom.
Help me stand boldly in the story You're telling.

PRAYER FOR JOY

God, show me how to laugh again.
Not the nervous laugh of survival—
But the full, free joy of being alive.
Let delight visit me again like an old friend.
Restore the dance in my step, even if slow.
Let joy surprise me like sunlight through clouds.

PRAYER FOR FAITH

I've doubted, Lord. You know I have.
But even in doubt, I kept whispering Your name.
Help me believe like a child again—
Not in perfection, but in Your presence.
Grow my faith where it's been bruised.
Hold my heart until it trusts again.

PRAYER FOR TRUST

I've learned not to trust many.
But You, Lord, have never failed me.
Teach me to lean on You again—fully.
Let me rest in the safety of Your plans.
Help me surrender, one fear at a time.
You are faithful. Remind me daily.

PRAYER FOR HER YOUNGER SELF

Bless the girl I used to be, Lord.
She did not know the storms ahead.
But she kept walking—brave and tender.
Forgive her her mistakes.
Honor her courage.
Tell her: *You made it.*

PRAYER FOR HER FUTURE

Whatever days I have left, Lord,
Let them be full of meaning, not just motion.
Fill them with gentleness, truth, and light.
Let the years ahead be lighter than the ones behind.
Give me peace in every breath forward.
And remind me: it's never too late for joy.

PRAYER FOR OTHER WOMEN LIKE HER

Lord, somewhere out there, another woman is breaking.
Let this story reach her before she falls.
Send my voice like a hand stretched out.
Remind her she's not alone.
Wrap her in comfort, hope, and clarity.
And walk her home to healing.

PRAYER FOR REST

Help me lay down what I've carried for too long.
Let my body feel what safety is.
Let my mind stop racing with regret.
Wrap me in rest that restores.
Let me finally exhale.
You are my Sabbath, Lord.

PRAYER OF PRAISE

You never left—not in the violence, not in the silence.
Through grief, through madness, through fear—You stayed.
I didn't always see You, but You were always near.
You rescued me in pieces, patiently.
Now I lift my hands not in defeat, but in praise.
I am still standing—and You are the reason.

EPILOGUE

I never thought I'd live to see this age.

I used to think healing would come in grand gestures. In reunions, or reconciliations. In redemption. Instead, it came in small moments. In the clink of a coffee cup in a quiet kitchen. In the feel of warm socks just out of the dryer. In watching a single bird return to the same branch every morning as if to say, *You're not forgotten.*

I wish I could say my children are completely whole. I wish I could say I am. But life doesn't always offer us that kind of ending. What I can say is this:

We have not given up.

One of my children—my sweet, deeply feeling child—has carved a life that looks functional from the outside. A good job. A small apartment. A cat. But there's a shadow that follows them, one that whispers in their ear that they could have done more. That somehow, the sins of their father must also rest on their shoulders. I see it in their eyes when we talk about Justin. The guilt. The pain. The need to protect even me from their own sadness.

The other refuses to speak of him at all. It's as if the story ended the day he left our house for good. Their survival mechanism has been deletion. I have learned to respect that boundary. Sometimes healing is choosing to never look back. I can't judge that. In fact, I envy it.

Justin died under a bridge. Not metaphorically—*literally*. A man who once memorized entire passages of poetry, who had the brightest blue eyes and once held our infant daughter like she was made of gold, died surrounded by damp concrete and the echo of his own mind. I do not romanticize it. I do not despise him. I simply mourn what was never going to be.

I remember the doctors saying he was "well enough" to come home. That he was "responding" to Haldol. That he "understood what had happened." I wonder if any of them read the notes in his file after he was discharged. If they knew he spent his nights staring at the children's bedroom door, whispering to himself. If they'd been there the night Spot—our loyal, beloved mutt—broke the spell of madness just long enough to keep me breathing.

I wonder if they knew how long it took me to sleep again without locking my own bedroom door.

I've lived decades since that night. I've moved homes. Switched jobs. Sat in too many therapists' offices to count. I've been angry at God. I've forgiven Him. I've been angry again.

But the one thing I never stopped doing was *trying*.

Trying to be a mother. Trying to be whole. Trying to believe that the world was not entirely evil, that somewhere beneath the rubble of my life, something sacred remained.

Some days it felt like I was crawling on glass just to get to bedtime. Other days, I felt the warmth of something divine—quiet, present, unearned.

Grace.

Not the kind you earn by being good. Not the kind you get because you went to church or volunteered at the PTA. The kind that finds you in the pit. The kind that sits on the floor with you when you're crying and says, "I'm not leaving."

I think that's what saved me.

Not a miracle. Not justice. Not even therapy, though I'm grateful for the ones who listened. What saved me was the slow, steady presence of a grace I couldn't manufacture on my own.

It was in the friend who dropped off soup without asking questions.
It was in the school secretary who held my child's hand when I couldn't get there fast enough.
It was in the woman at the grocery store who offered me a coupon and smiled like I wasn't invisible.
It was in Spot, my dog, who is long gone now but saved me in every way that matters.

Grace didn't make everything okay. But it gave me the strength to keep showing up. To keep mothering. To keep breathing. To tell this story.

And maybe—just maybe—that's enough.

I often get asked if I regret staying as long as I did.

It's a fair question.

The short answer? Yes.

The long answer? I did the best I could with what I knew at the time. I believed what the professionals told me. I wanted to believe in redemption. I wanted to keep my family together.

But if I could go back, I would leave sooner. I would trust my instincts. I would believe my children's fears instead of minimizing them. I would recognize that my love could not undo his illness, and that staying "for the sake of the family" was not noble—it was dangerous.

Still, I cannot rewrite the past. I can only speak it. I can only hope that another mother, somewhere, reads this and feels less alone.

I wish I could tell you that I've made peace with all of it. That

I no longer feel the shame, or the sting, or the weight of it all. But healing is not linear. And grief has a long memory.

There are still days when I hear something—a child crying in a store, a news story about a mentally ill man found in a tent—and my heart clenches.

I still carry the fear that I failed my children. That I didn't shield them enough. That they will forever associate childhood with danger.

But do you know what I hold onto?

That they're still here, too.

Damaged, yes. Scarred, absolutely. But they love. They try. They laugh. They move forward, even if it's slow. I watch them, and I am reminded that survival isn't always dramatic. Sometimes, it's just breathing through the next moment. Sometimes it's reaching for connection when your brain says to shut down. Sometimes it's remembering joy exists—even if you don't feel it right now.

A few weeks ago, I sat on my porch and watched the sun go down. The sky turned that impossible shade of lavender-blue, the kind that never lasts more than a minute. I thought of my mother. Of her warm hands. Of the way she used to hum when she cooked. I thought of my father, who always believed I'd be okay. Of my brother. Of the people I've lost—not just in death, but in memory.

I said out loud, "I'm still here."

It wasn't a triumph. It wasn't a battle cry. It was a whisper. A truth. A prayer.

I am still here.

And somehow, that's become enough.

If you've read this far, thank you. For bearing witness. For walking through the pain with me. For allowing me to tell a story that many would rather forget.

We live in a world that likes tidy stories. That wants to tie up suffering with a bow. But real healing is messy. Real trauma doesn't end just because the chapter does.

So if you're still grieving… if you still have nights when you cry in secret… if you wonder whether the damage done to your children can ever be repaired… I want you to know this:

You are not alone.

You are not a failure.

You are not beyond redemption.

You are still standing.

And that is no small miracle.

Grace doesn't always come in thunderclaps. Sometimes it arrives in the quiet.
In the breath you take before giving up.
In the heartbeat that says, "Try again."
In the whisper of a God who never left your side.

This is not the end of my story.
It's not even the middle.
It's simply a new beginning.
And by the grace of God, I will keep going.

BOOKS BY THIS AUTHOR

God's Design For Her (Grace For Every Season Book 1)

Find Strength, Grace, and Encouragement—One Week at a Time

Life is busy, but your faith journey matters. God's Design For Her: 52 Bible Verses for Women is a year-long devotional designed to uplift and inspire you. Each week, you'll find a carefully chosen Bible verse, a thoughtful reflection, and a heartfelt prayer—all created to help you grow in faith, embrace your God-given purpose, and walk confidently in His love.

Whether you're seeking peace, wisdom, or encouragement, this book will remind you that you are cherished, strong, and never alone. Take a few moments each week to draw closer to God and discover the beauty of His promises for you.

Start your journey today—because His grace is with you, every step of the way.

Angel Prompts: True Stories Of God's Gentle Presence (Heaven's Touch)

What if angels walk among us—unseen, yet unmistakably real?

Angel Prompts invites you into a world where the veil between heaven and earth is thinner than we dare imagine. These are not ancient myths or distant memories. They are raw, personal accounts—shared by ordinary people who experienced the extraordinary.

In these pages, you'll find stories of mysterious rescues, quiet interventions, unexplainable peace, and timely voices that could only have come from above. Each encounter is a powerful reminder: we are never truly alone.

Whether you're a skeptic or a believer, these true tales will stir your spirit, ignite your hope, and open your heart to the possibility that angels are real... and they're closer than you think.

The Angel Effect: Moments When Heaven Intervened (Angels In Our Lives)

Discover the Divine in the Everyday: The Angel Effect

We live in a world where some mysteries can be unraveled by science, logic, and reason—yet others defy explanation. These moments, fleeting yet profound, whisper of something greater: unseen forces at work, guiding, protecting, and comforting. Angels.

In The Angel Effect, step into a world where the miraculous feels tangible, where the extraordinary hides in plain sight, and where ethereal beings walk among us. Through deeply personal stories of awe-inspiring encounters, the author reveals a life shaped by faith and divine intervention. Whether it's a perfectly timed rescue, an inexplicable comfort in solitude, or a "coincidence" too perfect to ignore, these moments illuminate the profound presence of angels in our lives.

This book isn't about theology or doctrine; it's a heartfelt testimony of living in the awareness of something greater. The Angel Effect invites you to explore the possibility of a world where the impossible becomes possible and divine love touches every corner of existence.

If you've ever wondered about the presence of angels or felt the nudge of an unseen hand, this book will inspire and uplift you. Let these stories remind you that heaven may be closer than you think and that sometimes, all it takes to believe is to listen to your heart.

Are you ready to see the world differently? Embrace The Angel Effect and step into the extraordinary.

www.ingramcontent.com/pod-product-compliance
Lightning Source LLC
Chambersburg PA
CBHW061336040426
42444CB00011B/2950